(un)inhibited

m ennenbach

ISBN: 978-81-8253-741-5

First Edition: 2021
Rs. 200/-

Cyberwit.net
HIG 45 Kaushambi Kunj, Kalindipuram
Allahabad - 211011 (U.P.) India
http://www.cyberwit.net
Tel: +(91) 9415091004
E-mail: info@cyberwit.net

Printed at Repro India Limited.

For –

Maia and Dax – to the moon and back

N – I still haven't come close to describing you even after so many attempts. Every word is for you. I'll keep trying

Cerberus – World Domination boys, the game's afoot

River – this one is your fault

And to you, dear readers

Contents

thus the angel sleeps

years
of acid rain
have pitted
the ivory stone
from which
she was cast
yet never once
in her vigilant watch
has one of those
beneath her gaze
risen
yet
after so long
keeping guard over
the restless spirits interred
under her wide spread
wings
the facade begins
to crack
as even the most
virtuous
falls apart
and now the angel
sleeps
her stone tongue
pressed against
marble teeth
her long vigil
brought to end

as the stone
cracks
and only dust
remains

map of nowhere

i bedazzle my clothing
with panic buttons
in case of inadvertently
crossing paths
with other people
as i stomp my way
through
the mythological lands
of mirth filled
indignation
a dog eared copy
of the art of war
clutched tightly
in trembling hands
as the cold
of summer's shadow
breathes onto exposed skin
sending lines
of black clotted blood
to fill the map of nowhere

a hush filled night breaks day

the time
just before dawn
when the world
is still slumbering
the moon hangs
in pale white
dominion
the stars shine
like gems
long carved
from the ebon sky
this is the time
to reminisce
to fall back
into the fleeting
wakeful dream
of memory
where the walls
of the veil
are thinnest
between what was
and what could be
in this silent hour
the corridors
of the mind
are thrown open
to insightful
wandering
where the blockage

of the busy day
crumble
before
probing need

of mummification and bone trumpets

the ancient egyptians
would
lovingly remove
the internal organs
fill the cavity
of the corpse
with dried flowers
a hooked tool
entered
the nose
to extract the brain
then
with attention to detail
they would wrap
the body
in preparation
for the afterlife
in the duat
a year ago
i hit
the lowest point
of my life
in celebration
of this anniversary
i circle the drain
like
a deformed rubber duck
in the eye
of eternity

it feels as if
instead of using
dried flowers
my chest cavity
was packed
with fiberglass insulation
my brain
just stabbed
ineffectively
left to rot
in the cavernous skull
of ignominy
if this
is hell
it is about
how i
imagined
if not
the tortures that await
must border
on the profound
if this
is limbo
the constant din
of elevator music
is apropos
no matter
how hard
i scratch
the itch remains
vibrant
in intensity
no matter

how many
pills i dry swallow
the pounding
in my skull
plays on in a sped up version of the one two three four
ska signature mournfully
blown through
a bone trumpet

mist rising

the mist rises
gently
over the placid waters
thick
with algae
the world seems
stagnant
only the green
remains
only the green
remains
the stains
of life's last
refrains
bubble up
from the sewage
of yesterday
the sewage
of yesterday
stews
in primordial ooze
of proteins forming
rudimentary chains
with nucleocytoplasmic
integers
with nucleocytoplasmic
integers
from the sewage
of yesterday

only the green
remains
over the placid waters
still mist rises

growls

a drop of crimson
hits the surface
of the crystal clear pool
with a splash
sending ripples
across
the tranquil surface
before
dissipating
into nothing
a second
a third
soon
a constant flowing
stream
as the lone man
kneels shakily
trying to stem the tide
pouring
from his throat
to the side
she smiles
white teeth
with smears of blood
her tongue
runs
across her lips
as a shudder
of orgasmic pleasure

runs through her
i huddle low
in the brush
watching
my pulse
pounding in my skull
as i wonder
what happened
the insane lust
in her eyes
drawing me in
it is too late
for him
his life
spilled out
into the water
she is filled
with need
that calls to me
my hunger answers
with a low growl

bubbles

i long
for the tears
to fall
unfettered
down scruffy cheeks
to feel
the bubble
deep inside
pop
maybe find
just a few moments
of peace
from this
constant state
of
constantly stating
that every single thing
is fine
living
on the edge
of
a mental break
emotionally unavailable
to one's self
when
emotional immaturity
is the status quo
is difficult
at best

impossible to ignore
yet here
we sit
waiting
for a breakdown
to break down
the dam
holding the parts
of being human
that make
human beings
out of the marionettes
dancing
on the strings
of the unseen malaise
that drips down
the open throats
of happily working bees
that take root
in the hive
adjacent
to the heart

murder on the side of the road

as i drove
down
the empty highway
i witnessed
a murder
hovering
over the barren fields
circling
in preparation
of a meal
or so
i assume
the quiet drive
filled
with sudden
apprehension
as the black eyes
stared
with menace
at something
on the cold ground
far below
then
en masse
they swooped
a small rabbit
clutched
in the murderous
talons

as they flew off
as one
to feast
upon the tender flesh
of youth
i watched
in appreciation
at the smooth
strike
i witnessed
a murder of crows
and what
i can only guess
was the murder
of a little bunny
i kept my eyes
forward
after that
afraid
i was
an unwilling
witness
to the savage beauty
of nature

self distressed expansion

the universe slows down for me
in brief moments of clarity
these insipid seconds
stretch on and on
until all of infinity itself
can be boiled down
into a craven feeling
of fear and remorse
these singular instances
dance across the cerebellum
like sparks drifting
from a lightning struck tree
split in twain
deep in the forest
of dark shadows
creeping across
the leaf covered floor
where light is a memory
hidden in the bare canopy
of limbs vying for a taste
of the sun that has long since
turned away in vague disinterest
is it the first fat flake of winter
or just another ghost
touching the back of my neck
as i scurry about
in a false sense of necessity
seeking the things
that don't really mean anything

but all hopes are pinned on
having that secret buried deeply
that will unravel the mysteries
of why
of how
of existence
of making it from
one sunrise to another sunset
in a land forgotten
by the sweet touch
of earnest affection
spinning in place
to desperately affect the illusion
of moving forward
when all we do is sink lower
into the loose soil
of yet another daydream
turned bitter like the grapes
left to whither on the vine
the bones of the earth are hollow
devoid of marrow
as we tunnel ever lower
in hopes of popping out
the otherside
of this miserable boweevil
and moth ball infection
digging to the polar opposite
not knowing that it is mythology
science is just a set of rigid rules
that bend the hurtful act
of emotion
into back breaking insolence
with shivering limbs

and broken nails
we claw at the truth
to try and disfigure and recast it
into the lie we cradle
against heaving chest
as the spirits of fools
tickle our feet
and call it progress
it is a natural regression
this obsession with possession
when the demons we let in
are nothing but patterns
of self distressed expansion

lush lifelessness

john coltrane plays
a wistful riff
that echoes down
my flaccid soul
playing against
the vertebrae
introvertion
of another nightmare
left festering
across the sleepy
pockets of my mind
in daydreams like this
i know i am
just the soft piano
accompaniment
to the staccato high hat
that shivers
in the lulls
between notes
the back beat
to a symphony undefined
yet the saxophone
cries out an ode
to a lush life unseen
in the heady mire
of this infectious need
for more
of what there is
less and less of

dwindling stores
of necessity
my spine strung taut
like the strings
of the same piano
soaked with spittle
like the worn reed
discarded
among the last kiss
of the night before
another bit of litter
on the rainy streets
of tomorrow

contorted

this latest zeitgeist is one
of looking away
looking through
never really seeing
not caring
for anything
but keeping
the status quo
opinion
is only accepted
if it fits
the mold
the latest loudest
lamenters
find acceptable
all else will be decried
as hate
heads down
eyes averted
comply or comform
fit in or fall away
rethink every
second word
or risk
expulsion

deconstruction zone

i am
deconstructing
the remnants
of who i once was
so that perhaps
the marble facade
of willowy
understanding
might refract
the bitter rays
of winter sun
in reverse osmosis
injecting chlorophyll
into
the unnecessary bits
to overrun
the mitochondrial
subdermal hemotoxin
of hope
suffusing
the entire
cellular breakdown
with paisley daydreams
like rubbing your eyes
too hard
leaving the afterimage
of tapeworms
latched onto the inside
of eyelids

a promise of summer

as winter spreads
her crooked fingers
against the land
of sullen heat
the streams
along the highway
give forth
clouds of mist
that blanket the earth
between the trees
it looks haunting
to the three or four people
not so caught up
in their own
terminal velocity
angrily driving
to whatever destination
of no consequence
awaiting them
around the bend
i see you
spirit of the cold
with desperately
clawing grasp
yet i ignore you
with memories
of spring time bliss
playing on loop
in the dusty halls

of my mind
with swollen green buds
hanging
the promise
of summer glistening

sickness

she still
clutches my face
grabbing
with more ferocity
than is necessary
in a show
of love
more a sign
of ownership
left me shaking
sweating
through thirteen hours
of fitful sleep
yet still
she clings on
in a stranglehold
just south
of choking
just past
seeing spots
she is fever
she is pain
she is
we dance together
in these
awkward twitching steps
of sickness
a dance so macabre
this danse macabre

this bewitching act
of torture
draped
in loving admonitions
the natural response
to infection
an injection
of warfare
on the cellular level
to level
the playing field
of microscopic
quandary

iron pyrite sculptures

he built
monuments
to the monumental
failures
of thinking
the world owed him
anything
the chip on his shoulder
just a pebble
from the avalanche
of self doubt
leaving clouds of dust
with every
aching footstep
in the craters
of the giants
that came before him
from the valley of kings
there were no
preordained kings
just more
and more things
that never meant
anything
except to the fools
that worship
at the edge
of a cliff
as the ones

with understanding
pushed them
over the ledges
to pile up
with the bodies
of all those
that toiled before them
he carves
epitaphs
for those
that spit
epithets
while walking
with a hunch
from the weight
of the world
he puts on his own back
another fool
in a long line
of fools
that knew
just enough
to be dangers
to themselves
and those around them
worshipping kings
of nothing
while seeking
a pocket full of fools gold
iron pyrite sculptures
of the last line
of blank faced sheep
bleating

that the sky
is falling
when it is just
the lies of those
in power
trickling down

fetid glimpses of home

the splintering
of frozen trees
exploding
as the sap freezes
reminds him
of spreading his ribs
in a futile act
of showing
he has a heart
to those who don't believe
the echo
of the woodpecker
pecking
into the pulpy flesh
of the sullen tree
to nest within
reminds him
of drilling
into his skull
in an effort to let her in
he finds nature
an abominable thing
for all of the
concurrent woes
within
his fledging sorrow
yet he carves
across his skin
the dreamscene
of fetid glimpses of home

# of yesterday

the air felt stale
like in a tomb
sealed
for thousands of years
yet open
to the weak light
of a dying sun
about to go
supernova
and consume
the entire solar system
the ground
had long since dried
the fleeting remnants
of flora
as dessicated
as the smile
on an old whore's face
after years of service
in the cold back alleys
of the unforgiving
city
he sits on the bench
feeling the grit
in the air
across leathery cheeks
remembering
when it all seemed
vibrant

with a pained expression
of one who witnessed
hope die
on the winds
of yesterday

wink

he was
a self propelled grenade
of human instability
and insular anxiety
launched
in a headlong collision
with whatever
brick wall of doubt
was erected
along the narrow
arterial asphalt lane
lined with dreamshards
and razorwire of hope
airbags disengaged
seatbelts cut
impact imminent
a lackadaisical grin
as the last cigarette
sits between
clenched teeth
he aims
towards the center
hoping to spit
in the bullseye
of future neglect
with a fuck off wink
to the audience
just off camera

saturhaze

some saturdays
feel like freedom
while others
cast a pall
like a funeral shroud
over an otherwise
fleeting
sense of flight
the machinations
of grinding flesh
to paste
beneath
the mechanical jaws
of hubris
plays a catchy song
of bones splintering
along
the fluffy white
candy clouds
in the pastel blue
banishment
of weeping stars
hidden behind
the umbra
of nuclear malaise

oppenheimer

living
in the aftermath
of an oppenheimer
curse
pale horse people
kicking up the dust
of ashen cityscapes
winding the hands
on the clock
until the springs
are all sprung
the gears
as toothless
as any hope
for salvation
the ticking
of canary hearts
against the ivory cage
of ribbed excess
nothing
but the oily residue
of liquid bowel
evacuation
no sensation
or elation
no relation
lost in trans-mercurial
surface elastration
waiting

for the bright light
to bath us
in ineptitude
as we succumb
to the atom split
caught
in the flash bang
of electron drift
left to sift through
the piles
of what was once
love
blurred

blurry eyes
don't focus
like they once did
as the thunder
pounds
behind vacant stares
the world seems
bathed
in mirage
how do you calm
the storm
that seems
predetermined
to rustle
the vagrant stakes
of nonendearing
static
into a pulpit of shame
the light lacerates

the skin
of hopeless wonder
until all that sizzles
on the hot stones
is dead
to unseeing eyes
and darkness
is but a dream

devils

the devil
on my shoulder
got into the adderall
he is screaming
into my ear
the angel gave up
sent a postcard
from some
white sandy beach
in the fiji islands
leaving me
with little choice
as to which
direction to go
six six six
carefully carved
into the soft flesh
between my shoulder blades
where the stumps
of malnourished wings
once flapped
ineffectively
the dyslexic
little bastard
screaming
listen to those that
lived
rudderless
in the infernal seas

of seasoned souls
singing anthems
of avarice
to carry me
just at the surface
of this lake
of fire
dazed
in this smoky haze
of misunderstandings
doing what i'm told
like a good little soldier
regardless
of the tattered wisp
of once upon
a crime

entitlement

he wears
entitlement
like a cape
as he twirls
through the day
with nothing
but expectations
of agreement
to his every whim
a special brand
of tolerance
based on inherent
intolerance
to anything
that went against
his own set
of standards
unaware
he is an absolute
asshole

in the end of ends

he sits
wonders
if he vanished today
drifted off
with all the other
embers
of forgotten time
would anyone notice
or would he just be
another
faceless shade
lost forever
he clung so tightly
to dream
that when it crumbled
to become nothing but
more sand
at the bottom
of the hourglass
he was left
with nothing
but half moons of blood
from clenching his fists
to try and stop
the fading hope
he doubts it mattered
that he mattered
that any of it
was more

than a blip
on the surface
of eternity
yet
he cannot help
but wonder
at how painful it is
to see it all
fall apart
around him

the lazy artistic eye wanders

the smoke from the days last
cigarette stings the eyes of the
artist as he stares forlornly out
the window of the passenger car as
it bounces down the track
he doesn't see the world for what
it is or isn't just the way it
once could have been from the
myopic view of many sundered
sorrows spun in a hadron collider
the lazy eye of art in watercolor
swirls left to drip on the warped
wooden boards of a childhood home
that feels like a prison in the
vaults of yesteryear
the convexity of misapprehension
with a subtle glaze of too many
last calls spent searching for his
keys to serendipitous surrender as
the floor races to greet him
two glass eyes with a patch
painted with the skull warning of
the poisons he willingly ingests
as the sun sets on the afternoon
of his once promising career

new normal

welcome
to the new
normal
anxiety
depression
breathing in pollution
where you are
most likely
part of the problem
no one
has a solution
fill the scrips
pop the pills
forget the feels
settle
into the numbness
of the constant
barrage
of soundbites
retorts
replies
facts
are subjective
opinion
is fact
reality is surreal
the new normal
is yours
best viewed

from the bottom
of another empty
bottle

invertebrake the system

he is no longer able
to tell
which side
of the ice shelf
he is on
under
while slowly drowning
or above
suffocating
from cumulative fears
so he wills himself
to sink
to fall farther
from the rotten center
in which
he spends
his days
he wishes
he were a squid
boneless
color shifting
able to disappear
in a cloud
of ink
that way
the disappointment
of the daily grind
could do nothing
as he clogs

the gears
to make the machine
stop
with a sputter
of deep regret
for the many lives
turned to paste
in the mechanical
greed

bipolar opposites

i am
a screaming mime
a silent singer
painted into the frame
of the opposites
that engulf
my fragile
carbon core
with veins
of diamond
an arsonist
in firefighter garb
a surgeon
with numb hands
another blind fool
staring at the sky
wondering
why the sun
has yet to rise
my spine
is an ouroboros
consuming itself
as i lazily
roll uphill
against the curvature
of the flat
earth theory
that defines
irrational rationality

the sirens sing
into
my deafened ears
as i let
natural attraction
lead me into
disaster
unguided
as the mermaids
splash brine
against bare
nervous twitches

swimming with ravens

the words
are swimming
just out
of
reach
focus
is fleeting
lost
in the daze
of
the holidays
a coup
a coop
a loop
in lieu
of anything
making
any sense
the ravens circle overhead, beady eyes trained on the slow moving body leaving a trail of crimson across the hard packed earth
seven times seven times seven times seven the angels wept as the brass bell tolls hollowly over the sands of whispered lies

reality is the seedy underbelly of dream

the forest of thorns
drags across
the tender flesh
dripping poisons
that sizzle
upon
the brown grass
of tepid longing
infecting those
that stumble blindly
through the hellshit
of awakening
to rail against
the light of reality
piercing the hangover
of last night's
reverie
celebrating
the end
of one bastard day
to begin the next
in quick succession
a revelation
of revulsion
a reckoning
of recompense
all while muttering softly
this is not the life i chose

all that remained was hers

she wrote her fantasies across my
bare flesh with one long
fingernail dipped in the venom of
forever
i shuddered in spasms as the
paralytic took over my entire body
she purred in my ear as i
convulsed whispering every dark
dream she ever had into my willing
mind to play out across the canvas
gone blank with need
as the light beckoned in the
distance it mixed with her words
until eternity was nothing but
pain combined with the most
decadent joy
long after the flesh had cooled
her words traced deeper into the
fabric of who i once was
in the end all that remained was
hers

hindsight is 20/20, especially when the back-side is a 10

seeing her again
was like slipping on
an old pair
of glasses
the world was blurry
i felt out of my
field of depth
and in the end
i was just
nauseous
she was like
a trip
to the amusement park
at first it was wild
every ride
was something
to be enjoyed
remembered
experienced
then eventually
it was funhouse mirrors
distorting the truth
to fit
her narrative
as all
of my money
vanished
on fixed games

i consider myself
lucky
i escaped
with slight scarring
and a nervous twitch
some of the other
poor bastards
that fell in
with her
were never seen again
i'm not staying
she killed them
but her nails
are always red
and i never saw
nail polish
with the stacks
of make up
she used
to cover the real her
until that one morning
i woke up
figuratively
and literally
to realize
she was more
beast
than person
the pheromones
masking
the stench of decay

light

there is a moment
a singular
instance
when the stars
in the sky
shine only
for you
when the blessings
of the cosmos
send quasars
of indescribable
beauty
to reflect
on yours
in those
soft seconds
when your light
outshines
those
of infinitesimal space
all focuses on you

daydreams and landmines

she poured her heart onto the
paper with careless abandon, an
ambivalent amputation of the woes
that circumnavigate her sphere of
lonely sighs
the rainy season reminds of long
afternoons spent watching the
storms as we lay naked making
promises neither of us meant to
get to things we both desired
as the thunder sounds the charge
of the gates of hell falling and
lightning sizzles across her
delicate skin, i begin to question
everything with silent motion
she stares at her phone in post
coital boredom, waiting for the
next love of her life to randomly
text directions to the next
apocalyptic excursion away
yet her watercolors still bleed
through my tissue paper soul as
the sky cries blood for the wrath
of wounded lovers spending the
last moments lost in other's arms
daydreams are as dangerous as
landmines liberally buried with
the skeletons in the backyard,
because the maps we draw are

lessons in futility and brandished with lies
yet there are nuggets of truth,
like ore in the mud and filth of
languid sexual release, kernels of
doubt in the sea of belief, like
her fingers down my spine, they linger

sea swells and seashells and the salty mists of hell

if you were
to pin your hopes
to me
you'd see me
deflate
fly around the room
as the illusion
is broken
the inflatable fool
slouched
in the corner
i am less
than you think
than i wish
i am
the great whirlwind
of flaws
abandoned
since childhood
to dwell
with the other misfits
in the tall grass
beyond
roving eyes
an optical delusion
a tropical confusion
a less than
optimal extrusion

on an otherwise
pleasant day
as the sea swells she cocks her ear to seashells in the ever diminishing dream that oceans can carry her away, wash her clean, fill the places where sorrow jets in eddys in the tidal drift of nuance and new age incredulity
and her dead gaze falls onto the portuguese man o'war floating on the foamy caps promising naught but stinging no lashes not unlike the many others she has endured before in the tragic stage play she reenacts to a crowd of no one
a classic case
of the sea swells
the seashells
and
the salty mists of hell

a treatise on why bipolar artists overdose

there is this thing that if you don't have it you truly don't understand what it is
you may have experienced the edges of it, but it was a pit stop on the road, not a destination
it's called mania, it is pure speed and light and joy and wonder and your mind in perfect synch
it is perfection
it comes with a price
for every day of racing along in the world like you probably feel you should always feel
well
you've experienced this as well, even if you haven't been forced to follow demands of the mistress
it feels like your organs are coated with tar, but it sort of stings as it colors the grays
this lass is anxiety, she is the harbinger of the lady depression and is a bit of masochist
she likes pain
with her cool touch everything is off, something is wrong, whether you imagined it no matter what
then comes the full on depression like slipping into fireant pajamas for a cozy three week nap
so you are soaring
right
then you cannot tell in the sudden fog if there is a tree around the bend and you know there is
ultimate high denied
and depression isn't i am sad and want to cry, no no no it is i cannot get up and i hate myself for it

i need to do things
i do
i won't because i cannot and i cannot say why i cannot because i can't bring myself to
okay
shower? meh
food? meh
leave the house?
fuck right off
so why do we tend to overdose?
we chase that high to avoid that low and it becomes an endless cycle of masking the symptoms
then you are rock bottom to the tenth degree and you cannot find the memory of the high
what always helps?
drugs
what never helps?
drugs
but it sure feels like it
until it doesn't
and then it all feels like nothing
creation, something so effortless at the mania is now right behind a thin pane of diamond
so drugs let you take it and half heartedly make it again
until you need more and more to maintain that razors edge you run like an exhausted chimpanzee
some quit in time
some find the balance
a lot overdose because it is better than nothing, the nothing, her nothing but a royal we kind
and then it's done
thank god
this isn't a cry for help
it's casual conversation while drowning

turtle (s)hell

the turtle floats
mindlessly
one
with the cosmos
around it
buffeted
by the solar gusts
it's painted shell
a work
of true beauty
glistening lights
reflecting back
into the void
of space
a reciprocating
pulse and hum
of phases
the turtle
is tired
millennia spent
with the burden
of ungrateful life
gently spinning
around the heart
of the sun
it's bones
slowly mined
refined
made into

implements of war
that rage
endlessly
along the curved
shell
there is no
concern
what happens
should the turtle
expire
as all float
with reckless abandon
yet no
concept
of the stakes
it isn't
the end of the world
as we know it
no
just life itself

some mornings

the rain falls gray on a backdrop
of gray on city of gray in a
morning of fog where the world is
still sleeping in for lack of want
to swim in the dingy gray
these moments make my heart seize
up in my chest as her red lips are
the only color i can recall as the
rest of the colors swirl down into
the overflowing gutters
the coffee sends steam into the
cool air as the rain beads up on
the glass, between sips i pick the
drops out as they race downdowndown,
hoping to pick a winner
chaos effect ruins any hope, they
follow jagged paths like the
forked tongues of lightning that
occasionally flash above
it's too damn dark to be so damn
early, consumed by a lack of
color, a lack of emotion, a lack
of anything except dour disbelief
and modest dejection
yet somewhere out there, i can see
the pink tip of her tongue run
along those lovely lips and it is
impossible to not dream that they
are pressed against mine

the feel of her tongue running on
my lips to move like the raindrops
down the glass door that leads
into nothing but the whirling gray
of my soul
some mornings are met with fire,
with purpose, with need, while
others are sidewalk chalk drawings
swept away by the cold rains of
indifferent storms raging behind
hooded eyes

common divinity

been forgotten
the ill gotten
gains
of the rotten
nectar of ambrosia
spilled
from the trembling lips
of divinity
to slither
across the land
like serpents
of desire
my mind aches
yet
it pains me
to medicate
to deviate
to contemplate
a world where
the agony
doesn't linger
like the last
listless kiss
of love
gone to coal
i am inebriated
on
the foolish wonder
of misanthropic

ideals
of mass appeals
of journeying
into the surreal
to find
one last bastion
of common sense
in a land
devoid
of anchored
thoughts
a plethora
of like minded
individuals
subverting
individuality
to stumble
inadvertently
into the warm confines
of hive mind
brutality
as the sycophantic
hoardes
cry for blood
in the very same streets
they caroused
as youths
freely

monster

how much
of the real me
is too much me
for the world
at large
to handle
as the porcelain mask
cracks
to expose
scarred skin
pent up lies
irreversible damage
inflicted
by weather
by hope
by dream
by love
by self
monsters are real
they hide
behind our eyes
whisper
little acts of horror
in the quiet
between screams
how much
of the demon
haunting
this skin suit

of coarse hair
and incorrigible smiles
is too much
for innocence
to witness
when
the pendulous crystal
rends the boundaries
of depressive reactions
to loose
the gas
of anxious inaction
who will see
the beast behind
hazel eyes
who will look away
as disgust
colors the air
around them

wilted elegance

the snow
crunches
beneath
the heavy footsteps
loud
in the silent
night
the sheet of ice
on the river
cracks
as the temperature
plummets
there is
a subversive
transience
in matter
when the air
seems to move
slower
as atoms
vibrate
out of sync
with
the desolate variance
in the end
all succumb
to the gentle
recurve
of lavish

lethargy
that drapes
across
the frozen ground
trounced upon
in wilted
elegance

there's a title in there somewhere, but i got lost in metaphor

when i supped
on the fruits
of youth
partook
in revelry
masked
my symptoms
with the cures
i employed
ambiguously
enjoyed
subjected and rejected
the inability
to see the trees
for the forest
of hieronymus bosch
poisoned
shrubbery
as i willfully
pulled
the jesus bolt
from the helicopter
as i cut
the tightrope
mid act
to do my best
tarzan howl
into the roughspun

netting
carefully concealed
in the plastic jungle
there was so much
thought
put into the bullshit
the heist itself
was forgotten
eight plot twists
in the past
there was a point
most likely

eons away

it's another
day
staring
at gray skies
in another
parking garage
in another
dead end day
of less than optimal
mental health
alone
craving
the comfort
of a shared
mindscape
in this insanity
of numbed
reality
press your lips
to mine
as the wobbly spin
of the globe
sends
the desperation
of a billion souls
screaming
for solace
into the empty void
of space

please
loneliness
is draped
over shuddering
shoulders
as time
loses all meaning
each second
farther
from the domain
of satisfaction
lost
in another spin cycle
drained
of color
each gaze
that of the fish
on the dock
flopping
ever farther
from the water
confused
at the closeness
that is eons
away

cue credits

the endless
sorry
the princess
is in another castle
routine
of running
across battlefields
in search
of peace
is the proverbial
dog chasing its tail
unsure
what will happen
when the damned thing
is finally
caught
spending
all the time
chasing phantoms
that it becomes
the pursuit
not the eventual end
is there any benefit
to ending the game
before
the credits roll
or is the role
the hapless hope
of seeing them
scroll slowly
into oblivion

ode in decomposition

i would pretend
to not hear her
so she
would have to say
my name
make incidental contact
send shivers
of pleasure
down my spine
with the way
her lips and tongue
formed the words
electricity
at the touch
of her fingers
so in the
heavy silence
of sorrow
the fear
of clinical necrophilia
has settled
into the fractured
remnants
of who i was
when i was
hers
as i find myself
still loving
the corpse

of who we were
when we were
something more
than an ode
in decomposition

new piece

the cigarette sits smoking in the
glazed ceramic ashtray on the dark
wooden table
a glass of amber whiskey sweats as
the three ice cubes slowly melt in
the hot summer air
the sound of miles playing softly
in the background punctuates the
sounds of the busy street outside
he sits in a yellow sweat stained
sleeveless shirt on the couch
hunched forward to tap the keys
a halo of smoke shimmers around
his head like a benediction to the
words he feverishly types
his foot taps to the music his
mind cannot recognize in the din
of full creation mania
he paused the incessant clatter
for a moment and wipes his brow
before taking a long drag
the exhale of blue smoke stings
his eyes as he runs the cold glass
over his forehead slowly
a humble of voices carry into the
room with exotic accents raised to
the edge of violent dissent
he smiles as he takes another drag
before crushing it out in the

overpiled graveyard of butts
without thought he leans forward
again and the typewriter seems to
adopt the rhythm of the song
it may be no masterpiece slowly
coming to life on the blank sheet
as it winds through the rollers
but as he rips the sheet out and
carefully examines it while
lighting a fresh smoke he nods
sometimes the greatest works
aren't born of beauty at all but
out of those moments between

far from prying eyes

i have never seen a gigantic squid
but that doesn't stop me from
dreaming about the hunter in the
inky black
i have never ran my fingers
through the rings of saturn but i
can feel the icy drift on my
fingertips in the quiet
so many illusions, delusions,
intrusions, a mass confusion in a
life of destitution devoid of
grasping unto dream
yet between moments of chaos and
terror there lies a sublime
waveform that drifts the shackles
of reality away
there is why my quiet heart lies
beating on a bed of rusted nails
as life and hope sizzle on the
white coals beneath it all
and in the darkness the squid
swims laconically amidst the
frozen vapor of saturn far from
prying eyes of disbelief

i write

i write to you
in poetry
because the words
would stick
in my throat
if i tried
to say them
out loud
i write
to the world
in poetry
because
the feelings
are more
than i can leave
bare in the light
i write it all
in metaphors
so it muddies the waters
between lip and eyes
to maintain
a modicum
of dignity
in these trying poetic times

structural flaws

i used to think
i had a weak spot
for you
but over time
i realize
it is
a structural integrity issue
because
every time
you come around
i feel as if
i could collapse
i can feel
the void
in the basic
building blocks
of who i am
filled
with a deficiency
that can only be filled
by your presence
somewhere
in that mass
of double helix
there is
a random thread
magnetized
to your gaze
that begins

an unraveling
a cold shunt
in my forging
that leads
to cracking
a large crystalline pattern
in the matrix
of who i am
that begins
to shatter
when you vibrate
at that frequency
of yours
maybe
i am at my
best
when i am
falling apart
maybe
you are
the beginning
of my end
maybe
together
we can create
a beautiful wreckage
to scatter
across the land
or maybe
just maybe
you are
a protein
that fits

into my receptors
slowly starving
my cells of oxygen
while convincing
my brain
you are all
that is needed

fade

i have kept
my eyes
closed
this morning
clinging tight
to the remnants
of dream
my nose
flush
with her scent
my tongue
infused
with her taste
if i dare
open
my eyes
even
for a moment
i know
it will all
fade away

Also available by m ennenbach

From Potter's Grove Press
(un)poetic
(un)fettered
(un)collected vol 1
(un)requited

From Death's Head Press
Notches – A Collection
Hunger on the Chisholm Trail

Cerberus Rising
Cerberus Exploitation

m ennenbach is a poet in texas. a scribbler of tales, fermenter, father, and one third of Cerberus. mennenbach.com is home to daily poetry and updates.

www.ingramcontent.com/pod-product-compliance
Lightning Source LLC
Chambersburg PA
CBHW050022170726
48282CB00025B/508
* 9 7 8 8 1 8 2 5 3 7 4 1 5 *